Organizing Your Craft Space

Organizing Your Craft Space

Jo Packham

Sterling Publishing Co., Inc. New York
A Sterling/Chapelle Book

Chapelle, Ltd.
  P.O. Box 9252, Ogden, UT 84409
  (801) 621-2777 • (801) 621-2788 Fax
  e-mail: chapelle@chapelleltd.com
  Web site: www.chapelleltd.com

Library of Congress Cataloging-in-Publication Data available

Packham, Jo.
  Organizing your craft space / Jo Packham.
      p. cm.
  "A Sterling/Chapelle Book."
  Includes index.
  ISBN 1-4027-1602-8
1.   Handicrafts--Equipment and supplies.   I. Title.

TT153.7.P33 2006
745.5--dc22

                                                    2005024732

10 9 8 7 6 5 4 3 2 1
Published by Sterling Publishing Co., Inc.
387 Park Avenue South, New York, NY 10016
©2006 by Jo Packham
Distributed in Canada by Sterling Publishing
c/o Canadian Manda Group, 165 Dufferin Street
Toronto, Ontario, Canada M6K 3H6
Distributed in the United Kingdom by GMC Distribution Services,
Castle Place, 166 High Street, Lewes, East Sussex, England BN7 1XU
Distributed in Australia by Capricorn Link (Australia) Pty. Ltd.
P.O. Box 704, Windsor, NSW 2756, Australia
Printed and Bound in China
All Rights Reserved

Sterling ISBN-13: 978-1-4027-1602-7
      ISBN-10: 1-4027-1602-8

For information about custom editions, special sales, premium and corporate purchases, please contact Sterling Special Sales Department at 800-805-5489 or specialsales@sterlingpub.com.

Foreword

There are times in which I feel that I don't have time to take care of even everyday activities. Being a part of the sandwich generation with elderly parents, children, grandchildren, work, civic duties, and friends, I often get caught up and lost in everything that is going on around me.

One day, I decided to stop this runaway train on which I am a passenger and take a minute for myself. There wasn't any reason that I shouldn't be able to sit down and, for at least a few moments, concentrate on one of the many handcrafted projects which my company, Chapelle, Ltd., produces books about each month. So I took a "trip" to my paper crafting area, sat down behind the desk, and looked around. My room wasn't exactly in disarray, but it wasn't particularly in any order either. It took a few minutes of sorting through the accumulation of ads, memos, and knickknacks to find the supplies I was looking for. My break turned out to present more work for me, rather than any time of solace.

It was then that I decided to get my creative space into a well-ordered functional area once again. I began to formulate a plan for organizing my tools and materials, considering carefully all of the storage options that were available to me. And it occurred to me that there are probably thousands of women, just like myself, that need to take the time to

get organized in order to become inspired to actually create wonderful new pieces. So I decided to write this book that will guide you through the taxing process of reorganization, and that lays out beautifully organized spaces for seven different crafting medium areas.

It is my hope that this book will inspire you to take time for yourself, relax, organize, and create. You definitely deserve it!

Introduction 8

Chapter 1: Getting Started 10

Chapter 2: Stained Glass
and Mosaics 56

Chapter 3: Rubber Stamping
and Stenciling 66

Chapter 4: Scrapbooking 80

Table of Contents

Chapter 5: Paper Crafts 92

Chapter 6: Beading 110

Chapter 7: Yarn Crafts and
Needlework 122

Chapter 8: Quilting 130

Metric Equivalency 142

Index 144

Introduction

It is oftentimes extremely difficult, for most people, to find the peace and joy of the creative process in an unorganized, chaotic space. It doesn't seem to matter—as artists, crafters, or otherwise—whether we think of ourselves as organized or not. Even the most disorganized of us has a system. Regardless of that system, we oftentimes hurry to finish a project, buy something new and fail to put it away, or use our space for other projects. Our system then crumbles, leading to disarray.

Creating order may seem daunting, but it doesn't have to overwhelm you. Simply make the commitment to analyze and reorganize your work space, giving yourself appropriate deadlines and an organizational scheme that works for you. By taking these small steps, you are well on your way to being truly happy with the end result. It doesn't have to be the start of another year, the first of the month, the end of a big project, or after you quit your job. Any day is the perfect time to begin organizing your craft space.

Whether your project is large or small, it is my recommendation that you break it into smaller, more-manageable steps or stages. To successfully accomplish this task, each step should be reasonable enough to complete in the allotted time frame. Research has shown that a minute of planning saves five minutes of execution, making it an essential step in the reorganization process.

Begin by purchasing a tabbed notebook and a large calendar with enough room to make notes for each day of the week. Write the following headers on each of the tabs in the notebook:

• Plan of Action

• Budget Considerations

• Floor Plan and Space Options

• Storage Problems and Solutions

• Tools and Supplies

An organized calendar will have yearly events such as birthdays written in one color ink, important appointments and dates written in a second color of ink, and those dates that are somewhat flexible written in pencil.

Budget
Consideration

Floor Plan and
Space Options

Storage Problems
and Solutions

Tools and Supplies

Plan of Action

For one week, before you actually begin in your organizing, log each of your daily activities onto the calendar. Although this might seem mundane, it is actually very useful. Because time is such a precious commodity, it is oftentimes difficult to prioritize reorganization. However, by marking the calendar for a full week, you will notice time slots that are not filled with essential activities. By keeping such a log, it becomes apparent how much time is spent watching TV, running errands that could be consolidated, or simply doing nothing.

If you absolutely have no spare time to dedicate to organizing your craft space, simply get up a half hour earlier each day until the task is finished. If you are more of a night person, complete one daily chore before going to bed. Even with this seemingly limited time frame, eventually your space will once again be a structured area in which you will feel inspired, creative, and productive.

As you go through this chapter, you will formulate lists of errands and chores in each section of your tabbed notebook that need to be completed to succeed in your organizational endeavor. As each of these tasks arises, schedule them onto your calendar. Don't plan too much in a small time frame or attempt to organize every single day. This will inevitably lead to frustration, as you have other commitments in your life.

Tip:

Always mark your to-do calendar in pencil. If you do not complete a certain task on the scheduled day, erase it and write it in for a later date.

Decide how you would like to organize. Look at the big picture only long enough to break it down into more manageable tasks. Ask yourself these questions, and any others that pertain to your space, and record your answers in the Plan of Action section of your notebook:

- Will you tackle reorganization from top to bottom, bottom to top, or divide the room into sections?

- If tackling the room by sections, what will they be? (Worktable, desk, closets, etc.)

Once this has been decided, break it down one step further, and list what needs to be organized in each section.

- Will you clean out the drawers and the top of your desk?

Anna Corba, above left, Freddy Moran, above right, and Dee Gruenig, below, all have beautiful well-organized spaces for their respective crafts. To see details of Anna's organizational scheme, flip to Chapter 5: Paper Crafts. For organizing a quilt space, see more on Freddy Moran in Chapter 8: Quilting. Dee Gruenig's tips and tricks for keeping a rubber-stamping space clutter-free can be found in Chapter 3: Rubber Stamping and Stenciling.

- Will you rearrange your filing system?

- Will you add more shelves to your closet space to more easily access tools and materials?

- Will you move the furniture to create better flow?

- Do your smaller tools, such as pens, pencils, or adhesives, need to be separated and categorized?

If the task of breaking your work down into smaller sections proves intimidating, simply begin by creating a list of "problems" that need to be tackled.

- Are you constantly searching for elusive tools and materials?

- Do you consistently have to move something out of your way before you can work?

- Are the furniture, lighting, and tools truly what you need?

Remember that each craft or art medium has its own basic needs. To help you determine what those needs are, think about the order in which you actually create your projects.

- Do you work methodically, taking time to draw the concept onto paper, then gather the appropriate materials? Or do you sit down and gather materials as you need them?

- Do you work from right to left, left to right, top to bottom, front to back, or otherwise?

- Do you sit down, stand up, or a little of both?

- Do you have to go elsewhere in the house for additional materials or to find a better light source?

- Do you throw scraps away as you work, or do you let them pile up to be discarded once the piece is finished?

Lists are essential to organization and expanding your memory capacity. Writing down each of your tasks increases the chances that you will follow through. There is such satisfaction in crossing items off your to-do list.

At this point, your Plan of Action has all the information you need to create a better functioning work area. Now it is time to take the first step to correct what bothers you about your space. On the day that you plan to begin your organization, put an alarm clock or timer where you can easily see it and set it for the allotted time frame. Keep your notebook at hand so you can take notes and check off completed tasks. Turn off the phone, put a Do Not Disturb sign on the door, take a deep breath, and begin. You will be amazed at how good you feel about yourself, your work space, and your ability to create—not only at the end of the entire reorganization process, but with each small objective accomplished.

Tip:

Don't just keep a list of mundane chores. Keep a "fun tasks" list as well. If you are reading a magazine and see an advertisement for a new store, add a visit as an enjoyable task. You can also include project ideas on your fun list to motivate you to finish works-in-progress.

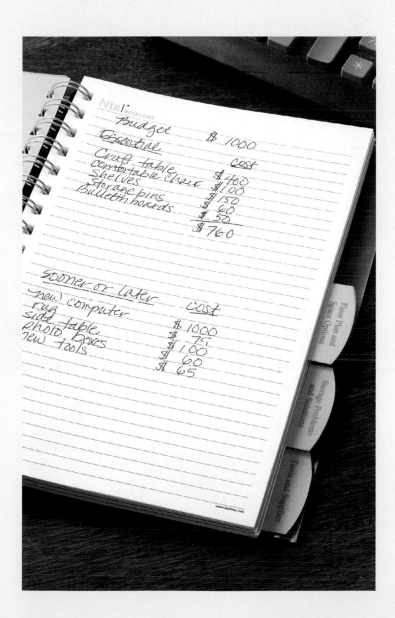

Budget Considerations

Whether you are planning a work space from scratch or redesigning an existing one, there are bound to be expenses. Buying or refurbishing furniture and equipment, painting, accessorizing, and updating existing storage are all important to creating a space you truly love and can create in. If you are on a limited budget, don't get discouraged. There are many ways to create your perfect work space without breaking the bank.

Begin by realistically establishing how much money you have to spend. In the Budget Considerations section of your notebook, create two lists of furniture and other changes you would like to make. The first list should include essential changes that take priority. The second list is for things that you would like sooner or later. Next to each item, write the estimated cost. Add up the totals of both columns and compare to the actual amount of money you have to spend. If your estimated cost outweighs your budget, there are many things you can do to compromise.

Pick items from your priority list that you are definitely going to purchase or change. If you aren't in a hurry, wait for the items to go on sale. Crafting and art supplies can be very costly. Make certain you understand what you are buying, its advantages and disadvantages, and how the price compares to other companies'.

Take note as you are shopping for tools and supplies, including such information as how much the product costs in various stores, whether or not the store offers delivery, if the product has a warranty, as well as the store's return, exchange, and refund policies.

Take a walk around your house and see if you already have unneeded or unused furniture that can be adapted to those you want for your work space. For example, a magazine rack can be made from an old ladder or the side of a metal baby crib. Be creative! Using your imagination can result in wonderful pieces. If you have trouble coming up with these kinds of ideas, flip through magazines or watch decorating shows on TV. They offer hundreds of ideas for making something out of nothing.

Decide on a figure that could reasonably be saved each week to buy those pieces that you can't afford right now. If you cut out lunch twice a week or make your own latte in the morning, you could save roughly $20.00 a week. Although this doesn't seem like much, it can add up to the necessary amount in a very short period of time.

Second-hand stores, flea markets, or yard sales are great places to find inexpensive pieces. An old door and four older windows can easily convert into a spacious worktable. All of the materials used can be inexpensively obtained from such sources as junk dealers.

"Trade" talents or items with a friend. For example, you could paint your neighbor's kitchen in return for a bookcase, or any other objects they might like to get rid of.

Organize this process by scheduling tasks on the calendar. List the dates by which your items can realistically be purchased, fixed, or created. To help the purchase time coincide with the organizational time, do them together in stages. For example, if you need new bookshelves, but cannot afford to buy them until next month, wait to organize your books until after the shelves have been purchased. Instead, spend this month painting, labeling, and organizing the items in your existing cupboards. If you coordinate your steps, the end result will happen much more quickly and affordably than you initially imagined.

Floor Plan and Space Options

Consider now if the space you have is adequate for the craft or art medium you practice. Size is not as important as organization and efficiency, because floor space can be maximized in a number of ways. There is no larger problem for a work space than a floor plan that does not flow, due to the fact that flow is the ability to have things at your fingertips when you need them.

Begin by asking yourself the following questions, and any others that pertain specifically to your space. Record your answers in the Floor Plan and Space Options section of your notebook.

- When is the space most used?

- Do you work only when there is absolute peace and quiet in the house?

- Do you view your space as a refuge for alone time, or do you prefer to share it with others?

- Is your space considered a family area where anyone is welcome to create?

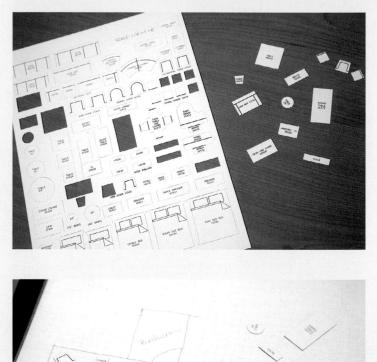

We are now going to create a floor plan on a grid. To complete this stage of the process, you will need the following items:

- Furniture cutouts or colored paper to make your own

- Graph paper, 12 squares per inch

20

- Pencil

- Plastic ruler

- Removable adhesive

- Steel tape measure

1. Begin by sketching your room on a sheet of drawing paper. Remember to indicate doors, windows, corners, permanent fixtures, etc.

2. Measure the walls and items indicated on your sketch. If your west wall is 12' long and 8' tall, record this on your drawing.

3. Double-check all of your measurements. *Note: It is easy to do this now, but will be costly if your bookcase or worktable doesn't fit later on.*

4. Transfer your sketch to graph paper. Using the squares as a guide, draw the room to scale.

5. Make several copies of the grid, so you have a replacement if it is lost or need to take it with you on a shopping trip.

Make a list of things you consider to be absolute essentials for your work space. Some of these items may be universal, regardless of your craft, but others may need to be adapted according to your particular needs. Your list may include some of the following:

- Desktop or work surface. *Note: An adequate size is generally considered to be a minimum of 36"x48".*

- Filing cabinet or other filing system

- Lighting and power

- Shelving

- Wall space

Do not forget to include large pieces of equipment, such as cutting devices, sewing machines, computers, or personal items that make your work more enjoyable, such as a television, stereo, or fountain. Buy or create cutouts for each item you have listed. *Note: Remember, these cutouts will be placed on your grid, so make certain they are to scale with your room.* Place the cutouts on your grid where you think you might like them in the room.

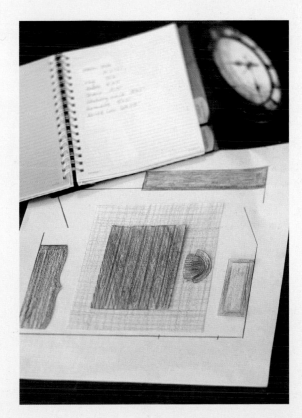

Using a red or yellow pencil, lightly mark the areas above doors, above or below windows, and underneath tables. This is space in which you could potentially place smaller storage receptacles or that could be used to add personal bits of decoration such as photographs or inspirational pictures.

Indicate with a different pencil color where electrical outlets are and plan accordingly for extension cords and power strips.

It is important to make certain, from the very beginning of your planning, that your work space is safe for you, your family, and your visitors. If your craft or art requires the use of hazardous materials, plan for cabinet space that is either locked or out of reach of children. Make certain wire racks can be secured to wall studs so they cannot be pulled out, and that nothing on the floor can be a potential stumbling hazard. Electrical cords should never run across walking areas, near water, or be where children can reach them. Planning for them wisely will help prevent future accidents.

Recommended Spacing Allowances

The following measurements will help you maximize your workroom space while allowing for ample moving room.

(This page) Utilizing "dead space," such as the area below desks and above windows, can add a plethora of storage space in any size craft room.

Desks should always be placed so that you are facing the door to avoid negative energy and allow harmony to flow throughout the room. Leave at least a 36" space for standing room behind the desk while opening drawers, and 42"–60" for pulling your chair out.

The area between desks, cabinets, and self-contained equipment with no drawers should also allow a 42"–60" pathway to accommodate all guests that may be invited into your craft area.

Areas with heavy foot traffic should allow 36" walking room, while 24"–30" in seldom-used areas is ample.

Always leave room in front of closets and bookshelves to easily view the contents. A good guideline for furniture with sliding or folding doors is 36", while the width of the door will suffice for pieces with swinging doors.

Depending on your craft, you will have a particular work surface. Whether you use countertops, a desk, or a table, consider placing glass over your work area so the surface remains in good condition. It is easy to clean and allows you to place favorite designs, note cards, pictures, or a calendar underneath for easy viewing.

(Left) The space behind the desk allows any visitor to browse the bookshelves without feeling crowded. Also, the top shelf maximizes space by placing trinkets and less-often read books out of the way but within view for inspiration.

Now is a good time to decide on a style for your craft area. There are two key points when considering how to decorate and which colors to use: 1) your own personal likes and dislikes, 2) what type of work will be done in the space. The color of a room can certainly affect the outcome of your projects. The following assessment will help you determine the best decorating style for you.

Decorating Style Assessment

When taking the test, be as honest as you can. Do not think about the answers. Simply mark the description that you instinctively feel best describes you. If none of the descriptions in the group are appropriate, leave the question blank. If there are two or more descriptions that you feel portray exactly who you are, mark each of them.

Finish this statement with the most accurate description: "When decorating my home, I . . ."

1. ___ A.   prefer intimate settings
   ___ B.   want my home to be a party home
   ___ C.   feel personal touches are not important in decorating
   ___ D.   want a private sanctuary

2. ___ A.   favor a simplistic style
   ___ B.   live a flamboyant lifestyle
   ___ C.   feel my work is very important
   ___ D.   need my spaces to be clutter free

3. ___ A.   feel having things is not important
   ___ B.   prefer nonstop shopping
   ___ C.   prefer to use a designer rather than do it myself
   ___ D.   am detail oriented

4. ___ A.   prefer casual decorating
   ___ B.   am artistic
   ___ C.   desire an uncluttered look and feel
   ___ D.   enjoy traditional decorating

5. ___ A.   prefer 100% cotton materials
   ___ B.   love brightly colored vinyl tablecloths
   ___ C.   would choose leather sofas over more practical options
   ___ D.   want comfortable materials

6. ___ A.   enjoy country living
   ___ B.   dream about city living in a loft
   ___ C.   prefer to live close to work
   ___ D.   love old houses

7. ___ A.   like nurturing spaces
   ___ B.   avoid having tiny rooms
   ___ C.   need a home office
   ___ D.   admire specialized rooms

8. ___ A. lean toward pleasant colors
   ___ B. enjoy vibrant colors
   ___ C. have sophisticated color choices
   ___ D. avoid loud colors

9. ___ A. choose modest furnishings
   ___ B. want my furnishings to make a statement
   ___ C. want furnishings that are influenced by modern styles
   ___ D. love antiques

10. ___ A. want my things to be made of natural materials
    ___ B. want everything to be unexpected
    ___ C. insist on integrity of design in my furnishings
    ___ D. need pictures to be in frames

11. ___ A. need rooms to be useful
    ___ B. feel rooms must make a personal statement
    ___ C. prefer minimalist decorating styles
    ___ D. think rooms must have a focal point

12. ___ A. decorate with the seasons
    ___ B. decorate for constant stimulation
    ___ C. decorate with balance and order
    ___ D. like period decor

13. ___ A. dislike new things
    ___ B. love unusual things
    ___ C. love gadgets and machines
    ___ D. prefer European-style furnishings

14. ___ A. like unpretentious accessories
    ___ B. choose accessories that are not routine
    ___ C. prefer accessories such as powerful paintings
    ___ D. prefer to swag, cloak, and cover everything

15. ___ A. desire a laid-back lifestyle
    ___ B. am always active
    ___ C. like a regimented lifestyle
    ___ D. favor family life

16. ___ A. enjoy collecting and displaying sentimental belongings
    ___ B. am a trendsetter
    ___ C. often prefer the idea of too little
    ___ D. feel some collectibles are "look, don't touch"

17. ___ A. prefer handcrafted pieces

___ B. prefer decorative items that can be handled

___ C. choose decorative pieces of the highest quality

___ D. tend to buy delicate, lovely things

18. ___ A. love wicker

___ B. choose leopard print over traditional fabrics

___ C. love glass objects

___ D. prefer soft sofas

19. ___ A. dream of having a greenhouse

___ B. want a home theater

___ C. want an elaborate aquarium

___ D. want a solarium

20. ___ A. need a room for relaxing

___ B. need a room for entertaining

___ C. would hide a wet bar behind a wall in the family room

___ D. want all the conveniences

21. ___ A. am a do-it-yourselfer

___ B. like regional or theme pieces

___ C. enjoy being surrounded by high-quality pieces

___ D. choose practical over frivolous

22. ___ A. feel texture is important

___ B. think patterns should be interesting, not just coordinating

___ C. prefer smooth sleek surfaces

___ D. like rich polished wood

23. ___ A. choose old brick walls over new drywall

___ B. would paint my rooms a mixture of colors

___ C. would make a hidden electronics storage unit in a wall

___ D. want elaborate moldings in every room

24. ___ A. need surroundings decorated with harmony

___ B. prefer an eclectic group of furnishings

___ C. fill my surroundings with museum-quality pieces

___ D. enjoy being in the lap of luxury

25. ___ A. prefer bare windows to drapes
    ___ B. design my own window coverings
    ___ C. choose expensive wood blinds as window covers
    ___ D. feel windows should be opulent

26. ___ A. surround myself with houseplants
    ___ B. have interesting sculptures instead of plants
    ___ C. would have a magnificent orchid
    ___ D. choose fresh cut roses instead of plants

27. ___ A. would have barn wood floors
    ___ B. would choose mosaic or tile floor coverings
    ___ C. would have marble floors
    ___ D. prefer oriental carpets

28. ___ A. cover the bed with squashy, comfortable pillows
    ___ B. like batik pillows on my bed
    ___ C. do not like pillows on my bed
    ___ D. adorn my bed with tailored pillows

29. ___ A. prefer comfortable chairs instead of stylish ones
    ___ B. need my chairs to make a statement
    ___ C. prefer chairs as art
    ___ D. prefer fainting couches instead of chairs

Totals: ___ A. ___ B. ___ C. ___ D.

Interpreting your score:

Mostly A's=Idealist

Mostly B's=Adventurer

Mostly C's=Leader

Mostly D's=Guardian

Tip:

If you can't decide on a style or design for your space, find a new muse. Tour local art supply, knitting, paper, and needlework stores. Notice how they categorize their products, display tools, and organize their books. Ask a knowledgeable sales clerk what works in regard to their organizational plan and what she feels could be improved upon.

The Idealist

Natural and simple describe your ideal setting. You do not need a lot of "stuff" to make you happy, although the items you do have are generally sentimental. Pictures of family and friends, art objects given on special occasions, or trinkets from your children are your preferred collectibles.

Cotton is the most suitable textile for your craft area, and an overstuffed leather chair would make a nice addition for time spent searching through magazines or for accommodating guests. You might prefer to refurbish used furniture rather than purchase new items, which works well, as you probably don't mind if your furniture matches or not.

Live plants and fresh flowers will give your space a clean-feeling atmosphere, which will, in turn, stimulate your creative mind.

The Adventurer

An eclectic mixture of various styles and colors works well for you. Modern furniture and funky patterned curtains or rugs will make you feel right at home. If you would like to accommodate guests in your work area, a dark red leather sofa might be a good option, or a larger worktable if your guests are interested in working alongside you.

The walls in your craft area will most likely be painted a variety of bold colors and the more diverse accent pieces, the better. Inspiration will come naturally if your environment contains an abundance of fun and interesting objects.

The Leader

An orderly space with time-saving conveniences and matching traditional furniture suits you best. Quality and design are your top priorities, while recessed lighting will give you the desired look for your work space. A chrome-and-glass table or a mahogany desk will serve their function while giving the room a pristine, classy feel. Neutral walls complement your style, with splashes of color found in the nicely framed, carefully selected artwork.

The Guardian

Subtle lighting on rich wall color and elegant antique furniture will be the mainstay in your craft space, which also functions as your private sanctuary. Ornate, gold-leaf picture frames are becoming as they surround the art within, and an abundance of bookshelves hold the works that inspire you. Small accent pieces, such as tassels hanging from doorknobs, help arouse your artistic inclinations. A storage system with many small drawers and hidden compartments is an essential for your craft area.

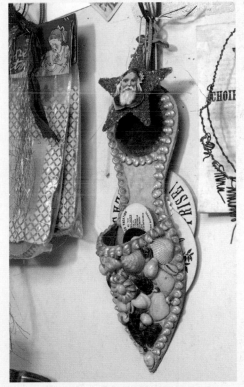

Decorating styles are closely linked to individual personality traits because both are representative of who you are. By comparing your personality type to your decorating style, you will be able to determine if they are equivalent, or if your tastes flow into two or more categories. If this is the case, try to incorporate all aspects of your personality and decorating styles into your craft space. As a great deal of time will be spent in that area, it is important that you feel comfortable there.

Personality Assessment

When taking this test, be as honest as you can. Do not think about the answers. Simply mark the description that you instinctively feel best describes you. If none of the descriptions in the group are appropriate, leave the question blank. If there are two or more descriptions that you feel portray exactly who you are, mark each of them.

1. ___ A. Emotional
   ___ B. Innovative
   ___ C. Versatile
   ___ D. Punctual

2. ___ A. Sympathetic
   ___ B. Enthusiastic
   ___ C. Rational
   ___ D. Agreeable

3. ___ A. Worried
   ___ B. Bold
   ___ C. Composed
   ___ D. Indecisive

4 ___ A. Analytical
   ___ B. Playful
   ___ C. Knowledgeable
   ___ D. Inventive

5. ___ A. Overly sensitive
   ___ B. Diplomatic
   ___ C. Opinionated
   ___ D. Tolerant

6. ___ A. Perfectionist
   ___ B. Values freedom
   ___ C. Decisive
   ___ D. Predictable

7. ___ A. Quiet
   ___ B. Sociable
   ___ C. Powerful
   ___ D. Reluctant

8. ___ A. Nurturing
   ___ B. Naive
   ___ C. Dominant
   ___ D. Dependable

9. ___ A. Suspicious
   ___ B. Happy
   ___ C. Curious
   ___ D. Contented

10. ___ A. Unsure
    ___ B. Charming
    ___ C. Assertive
    ___ D. Easygoing

11. ___ A. Sincere
    ___ B. Witty
    ___ C. Determined
    ___ D. Useful

12. ___ A. Compassionate
    ___ B. Spontaneous
    ___ C. Competent
    ___ D. Responsible

13. ___ A. Well-behaved
    ___ B. Impulsive
    ___ C. Impatient
    ___ D. Patient

14. ___ A. Respectful
    ___ B. Outgoing
    ___ C. Lacks compassion
    ___ D. Good listener

15. ___ A. Loyal
    ___ B. Optimistic
    ___ C. Honest
    ___ D. Kind

16. ___ A. Empathetic
    ___ B. Exciting
    ___ C. Logical
    ___ D. Diplomatic

17. ___ A. Detail-oriented
    ___ B. Prefers to party
    ___ C. Action-oriented
    ___ D. Shy

18. ___ A. Devoted
    ___ B. Easily bored
    ___ C. Independent
    ___ D. Accepting

19. ___ A. Reliable
    ___ B. Trusting
    ___ C. Demanding
    ___ D. Considerate

20. ___ A. Idealistic
    ___ B. Carefree
    ___ C. Pragmatic
    ___ D. Even-tempered

21. ___ A. Creative
    ___ B. Adventuresome
    ___ C. Capable
    ___ D. Traditional

22. ___ A. Poetic
    ___ B. Physical
    ___ C. Precise
    ___ D. Giving

23. ___ A. Disciplined
    ___ B. Competitive
    ___ C. Direct
    ___ D. Content to follow

24. ___ A. Thoughtful
    ___ B. Charismatic
    ___ C. Perfectionist
    ___ D. Avoids conflict

25. ___ A. Romantic
    ___ B. Uncommitted
    ___ C. Obsessed
    ___ D. Faithful

26. ___ A. Unrealistic
    ___ B. Learns by doing
    ___ C. Self-critical
    ___ D. Adaptable

27. ___ A. Judgmental
    ___ B. Undisciplined
    ___ C. Confident
    ___ D. Ambivalent

28. ___ A. Careful
    ___ B. Flexible
    ___ C. Insensitive
    ___ D. Resists change

29. ___ A. Future-oriented
    ___ B. A performer
    ___ C. Task-oriented
    ___ D. Practical

Totals ___ A. ___ B. ___ C. ___ D.

Interpreting your score:

Mostly A's=Earth/Blue

Mostly B's=Air/Orange

Mostly C's=Fire/Red

Mostly D's=Water/White

The color with the highest score reflects your natural personality. The number totals under the other colors represent the amount of that personality type that influences who you are.

The Earth Element or Blue Personality

Intimate and authentic, you value people and friendship more than obeying rules, having fun, being logical, or being right. Harmony and cooperation are important to you, as are strong morals and ethics. As a poetic, romantic, and devoted person, your space will reflect these qualities, and in many cases, you will be open to sharing your space with others in order to maintain a conflict-free environment.

The Air Element or Orange Personality

A spontaneous and free person, organization is something that does not come easily for you. Action, excitement, and immediate results are the key ingredients to your well-being; therefore, planning and structure hold little of your interest. You are very verbal and optimistic, and benefit far more from taking action than by listening to others. Your creative space will likely include impulsive purchases being put together on a whim.

The Fire Element or Red Personality

A natural leader, your strengths are power and knowledge. You are a very hard worker, and continually strive to be better than your best. As a seeker of new solutions, you will create a plan that works for you, and will follow through until your goals have been met. Your organizational endeavors will be undertaken in an analytical way, until each and every item in your craft area has a logical place to be stored.

The Water Element or White Personality

Tradition, family, and stability are highly valued by you. Predictable and punctual, you handle detail well and have the ability to make things happen. Your creative space will become a haven of order in due time; your own methods and timeline cannot be swayed by others. However, because you are efficient, responsible, and prepared, the task at hand will flow quite smoothly once begun.

Choosing Color Combinations

While decorating styles have a big impact on your work area, the colors you choose are also important.

Warm Tones

Warm colors, including reds, yellows, and oranges, create feelings of cheerfulness and vibrancy. High energy, warm tones can make rooms look slightly smaller, adding a sense of coziness. However, they can also create a sense of suffocation. If you view your crafting area as a room where passion and vigor ignite creativity, a room with more warmth might be a good option.

Cool Tones

Cools colors, including blues, greens, and purples, can induce calm and create a fresh yet soothing atmosphere. As these quiet hues recede, they can make a room appear larger and somewhat icy. If your craft time also functions as a winding-down period in your day, the placating effects of cool tones are a good option.

Neutral Tones

Neutrals, such as white, beige, or taupe, neither activate nor pacify emotion; they simply blend and cooperate. Some find neutral colors very bland but this can be avoided by adding accent colors to brighten and intensify neutral areas.

Storage Problems and Solutions

Now that you have a basic floor plan and an idea of how you would like to decorate your space, it is time to think about storage. Storage is an important consideration when finalizing decisions about furniture placement, or even what type of furniture to buy. Considering storage issues now will maximize the potential of your work space.

There are currently endless storage options available to you these days. Large, plastic storage bins are an inexpensive way to categorize tools and materials, while wicker baskets are attractive and don't need to be hidden from view.

Books

There are many ways that books can be stored and categorized. While shelves are the most obvious solution, you may not have room in your budget or space in your craft area for shelves to house all of your books. If this is the case, get creative with your storage. Utilizing the area beneath a window seat or workbench can take up some of the "dead space" so often found in work areas, while making the books easily accessible. Empty floor space can be a great place to stack books, as well as serve as a makeshift table for displaying cute knickknacks or fresh flowers.

Categorizing books should be accomplished according to a system that works for you. Generally, organization works well when books are placed according to author, title, or subject. Once you have decided on a main category, use subcategories to continue keeping items in a place that will make them easy to find. For example, if categorizing by subject sounds easy for you, break your shelves up into sections, such as knitting, painting, and scrapbooking. From there, you can subcategorize into general techniques: knitting hats, knitting sweaters, watercolor painting, painting murals, creating vintage scrapbooks, scrapbooking altered books. From there, the books can be placed alphabetically according to title or author.

Personally, I like to organize my books by color. Being a very visual person, I oftentimes can better recollect a particular book not by its title, but by the color of the book as well as the picture on the front. Books can also be stored by size, which creates a nice visual flow.

Bookends are a great way to accessorize a bookshelf that needs a bit of detail. Not only are bookends useful for keeping your books upright, they add personality to your shelves.

Magazines

If you like to save entire magazines, decide on your preferred filing method. You can file by title, year, then month, or by year, title, and month.

Magazines can be stored in filing cabinets, boxes, magazine racks, or binders. Any print shop can inexpensively drill holes in a stack of magazines. If you keep entire magazines but want to remember specific articles or ideas, mark them as you read using a color-coded system. For example, if you are a mosaic artist, mark garden ideas with green, furniture projects with blue, small gift items with red, etc. A "code list" posted in a visible area will help you remember which color is indicative of which category. Instead of self-adhesive notes, try photocoping those pages, and file them separately. Likewise, you can save and file only those articles, and discard the rest of the magazine.

It is important to the upkeep of an organized, well-flowing space to go through your magazines at least once yearly. Those that you no longer want or have not used should be thrown or given away. If you do not save entire magazines, keep a list of fellow crafters who might like to read those issues you no longer have use for. You might also consider donating them to a senior citizen home or a hospital.

Magazines offer all of us not only a source of inspiration but a moment for relaxation. By your favorite chair, keep your magazines organized and displayed in a wicker basket or favorite designer fabric-covered box. Also in the basket keep a smaller container with pens, scissors, paper clips, self-adhesive notes, and file folders. These will allow you to mark your magazines as you enjoy them. When you are finished, magazines and ideas can be filed for future reference.

Beads, Buttons, and Accessories

Many crafts involve tiny detail pieces that can easily get lost or jumbled together, creating further disorder in your work space. To resume order, separate small items into like categories. For example, divide your bugle beads from your seed beads, then separate each category of bead by size, color, and shape. Measure the dimensions of a drawer in which you would like to store your smaller objects. Purchase jewelry trays with several compartments, then line them with felt, making certain the trays are of the same dimensions as your drawer. As jewelry trays are usually about 2" tall, you can stack multiple trays on top of each other within the drawer for maximum space efficiency.

Tip:

Getting creative with your storage is a way to express yourself outside your art. Using flea-market finds, such as old glass sorbet dishes or vintage muffin tins, can keep supplies not only separated but on display for inspiration.

Ribbon

Ribbon can be stored in a number of ways. It can be sorted according to color and width then stacked on shelves designated to that particular color. A very decorative place to keep ribbon is right on your work surface, stacked on a vintage pastry rack. However, one of the easiest ways to keep ribbon very accessible is to place a few dowels in a rack on the wall. Slide the ribbon directly onto the dowels, as shown in the photograph bottom-left.

Tools and Supplies

The best way to organize your tools and supplies is to ascertain exactly what you already own. To do this, go through your drawers, closets, boxes, and other storage areas and make a list of all your items.

An easy way to list things is by titling separate sheets of paper with main categories, then creating subcategories for each list. For example, one sheet of paper would have "adhesives" as the category. Subcategories on this list would be divided into paper adhesives, wood adhesives, construction glue, etc. Actually going through all of your items can be done in one of two ways. You can pull everything out all at once, and arrange them on a tabletop or the floor before categorizing. If you have limited space, you may want to only go through like items at a time.

Once everything has been listed, divide the items into two piles. One pile is for things that you use and wish to keep, while the second pile is for things you are going to give away. Put everything that you will be giving away into a sack or box, and set aside. Divide the items to be kept into groups of items that are seldom used or items that are frequently used.

To avoid having to categorize your tools and supplies again in the future, try keeping an Inventory Notebook. This is useful both for remembering what you already have,

as well as for recording items that need to be restocked. It is as frustrating and time-consuming to run out of a much-needed material as it is to come home and find you have just purchased a duplicate of something you already own. Although keeping inventory might sound like a lot of work, it will save time, energy, and money in the long run.

Looking back over your list titles, determine what types of containers should be used to store your items, and write this information at the top of each list next to the category name. For example, pencils can be stored in a flat plastic bin, a vintage drinking glass, or bottle. Get a fresh stack of paper, and head each sheet with areas in which the containers can be stored. One sheet might be headed "filing cabinets," while a second sheet is headed "desk drawers" with the subheads "First desk drawer, " "Second desk drawer," etc. Decide which containers should be stored where, taking into consideration the sizes of the containers, how often the contents will be used, where placement should be in proximity to your work space, and how heavy they are.

Place all of your items into their designated containers. Clearly label each container before it is placed in your workroom, so that you can easily distinguish between them. Make certain your container is suitable for the item it will be holding. If the items are fragile, the container will have to be lined to prevent breakage. If the items are valuable, you will want a container that can be locked. If any of your containers have open holes or grids, such as a wire basket, make certain the items placed within cannot fall through.

Discard any items that are no longer necessary. There are many ways to dispose of unwanted tools and supplies without creating excess waste.

• Donate items to a church, hospital, senior citizens group, or school.

• Give unused items as birthday or Christmas gifts by making a gift basket. Used items can be given to your children or other family members who would enjoy them.

• Have a swapping party with friends or other crafters. Make certain you have a table that is large enough to display all of the items, and that each item is labeled with the owner's name to ensure equal return on trades. If you don't have time for a party, trade online.

• Sell items at garage sales, flea markets, or on the Internet. It is worth your time to do so if you have many items to sell or if it is expensive machinery.

• If items are of no value to anyone, throw them away. Make certain

potentially hazardous materials are properly disposed of by checking with the manufacturer or your local recycling center.

General Organizing Solutions

Arrange by Category

It is generally easiest to find items if they are stored with items of similar size, shape, or function. For example, keep all of your colored pencils in one small container, your writing pens in a second similar container, and specialty pens in a third. If all three containers are placed in the same area, they will always be easy to find and access.

Drawer Space

Dividers can actually create more space in a drawer if utilized properly. Traditional portioned kitchen trays can be used to organize brushes, pens, or pencils instead of forks and knives. Make certain to not cram too many items into one tray, however, or they will spill into other containers or create a drawer jam. Also, remember to leave room for newfound treasures, or you may have to reorganize again. If you are stacking bottles of ink or dye, consider lining the drawer with contact paper, thin protective rubber, matte board, wrapping paper, or other protective lining.

Shelf Adjustment

If your cabinets have movable shelves, make certain you take full advantage of their flexibility. Place your tallest items on the bottom shelf, and use them as a guide for placement of the next shelf. Make certain your most frequently used items are placed on the shelf that is easiest to see and reach, and that shelves are strong enough to indefinitely hold heavier items.

Maximizing Cabinet Space

Racks, holders, and fixtures that hold supplies inside your cabinet should be used whenever possible. For example, you can purchase a special glue-gun rack that attaches to the inside door of the cabinet, thus saving shelf space for other materials.

If your cabinets are deep enough, consider installing a lazy Susan to maximize space at the very back, while retaining easy access.

Dividers can also be purchased to separate cabinet space vertically. These are very helpful when storing such items as matte board, large cutting sheets, or frames.

(Below) These bottles are neatly lined up in a desk drawer. This way, the labels are easy to see without having the bottles constantly in the way. For more on Drawer Space see page 47.

Stack Wisely

Whether you choose to use vintage cigar boxes, plastic bins with drawers, or other storage devices, you will probably need to stack them to maximize your space. Stacking, however, poses some problems, especially if your containers have lids. It can be frustrating and time-consuming to restack boxes when what you need is at the very bottom. Here are some points to consider when purchasing stackable storage:

- Containers with drawers are the most accessible, but are also the least decorative.

- Square containers use less space than round ones

- If you are using multiple containers for your items, remember to label or attach a photograph to the outside of each one so the contents are known without having to open the box. If the contents inside have a shelf life, such as glues that become unusable after awhile, date the box as well.

- For further organization, stack boxes by size or content. Another solution is to keep similar supplies in the same color boxes. For example, keep all of your cutting tools in green boxes and drawing tools in cream-colored boxes.

49

Wall Storage

Employing your walls can more than double your storage area. Paint pegboards and use them to hang various tools and items. Hang funky hooks in rows and fill them with cordless tools, ribbons, or trims. Rain gutters can be attached to the walls for holding spools of thread or ribbon, while metal flowerboxes can be filled with bottles or smaller boxes. It can even be cost effective to build a second sliding wall to create surfaces large enough to house works-in-progress. Used with runners, a sliding wall moves back and forth to reveal a large painting or quilt that can be worked on when you have time, while the outer wall serves as space for a second project, as shown in the photograph at right.

Every workroom should have a bulletin board. If you need one larger than those found in the store, try covering the wall with a few layers of cork, or cover a piece of cork with decorative fabric, and insert into a vintage picture frame. Tin sheets or special metallic paints result in a pleasing magnetic board. Using the entire wall as a bulletin board creates a vast amount of space that can be used for storing as well as decorating. If space is limited, a memo strip can be purchased or made, as this type of space is essential for posting important notes, calendars, photographs, or other inspirational items.

(Right) This magnetic wall was coated with metallic paint and is an inexpensive way to make your entire wall function as a bulletin board. Adhere your favorite photos to the front of flat magnets.

(Opposite, top left) These decorative clips can be secured directly to the wall. They are a great place to keep important reminders, while keeping them off your work surface.

(Opposite, bottom left) This mini-bulletin board is not only decorative but functional. Part of the board is magnetic, allowing you hang business cards, photos, or advertisements, while the notepad allows you to scrawl any messages or reminders.

(Opposite, far right) This bulletin board, in Anna Corba's studio, covers the entire wall.

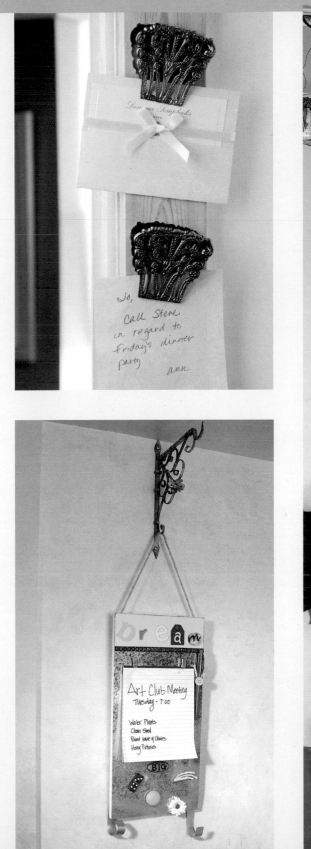

Jo,

Call Steve
in regard to
fridays dinner
party
ann

br*e*am

Art Club Meeting
Thursday - 7:00

Water Plants
Clean Shed
Paint table & chairs
Hang Pictures

Ceiling Storage

Don't discount your ceiling as an excellent place for storing things. While a pot rack traditionally goes in the kitchen, one can also be used to hang dye pots, candle-making pots, or measuring containers. Wire baskets can be hung for holding a variety of tools and supplies while vintage ladders are great for drying flowers or dyeing ribbon.

Counter Space

No one ever seems to have enough counter space in his or her work area. If your space is not large enough to build additional counters or an island, consider foldout tables along one wall or from behind a door. Remember to only keep essential items on countertops, as stacking magazines, mail, or found treasures will result in unnecessary clutter. If you have a sink in your workroom, have a cutting board made to fit over it. This will add to your counter space when the sink is not being used to run water.

If family or guests are often invited into your space, make certain there is ample room for everyone, as well as two sets of tools and supplies. If they choose to store their own tools and supplies in your work-room, make certain they are clearly labeled to avoid mix-ups.

Organizational Maintenance

Daily cleanup is essential to maintaining a well-organized, inspirational space. Here are some tips for preserving your newly organized area:

- When beginning a new project, always make certain to create a new file to go along with it. Once the project is complete, clean out the file, throwing away anything that is duplicate or no longer necessary.

- Filing ideas for projects can be done in a number of ways. You can file by category (knitting, painting, decorating), end use (gift, personal, gardening, decoration), or holiday/occasion (birthday, Christmas, anniversaries). In each of these files, create subcategories such as "Projects to complete immediately," "Favorite projects," or "Important projects."

- File every day. Either set aside five minutes at the end of your crafting session, or file things as they come up in order to avoid a lengthier filing session in the future.

- Every scrapbook maker knows the frustration of trying to find a particular photo amidst hundreds. As soon as you pick up your photos, make it a point to record the date and/or special event on the outside of the envelope, as well as who, what, when, and where on the back of each picture.

- Throw trash away while working to avoid extra clean-up time. If your space allows, buy more than one trash can so there is always one nearby. Keeping extra liners in the bottom of the can is useful for quick replacement, as is having one large can to empty each of the smaller cans into. If you like to save your scraps, keep both a trash can and scrap receptacle handy.

Of course, daily cleanup isn't always your top priority. To avoid returning to clutter, designate one day each month to clean and reorganize your space. Mark it on your calendar and make certain to keep your appointment, the same as you would if meeting friends or attending a meeting.

Tips for Healthier Crafting

- Take a 10-minute break every 50 minutes and vary your activities. Changing patterns stimulates the brain, increasing productivity.

- Support your lower back with a pillow or rolled-up towel when sitting for extended periods of time. Lumbar back support is imperative to maintaining good posture and alignment.

- Keep your forearms level with your work space. If your workstation is too low, it will hurt your neck and back. If it is too high, your arms will tire and your neck muscles will become strained.

- Good lighting can increase productivity from 10–40 percent, while decreasing eyestrain, headaches, and mistakes.

- Make certain your ventilation system is appropriate for your craft. Good ventilation is more imperative in a craft in which many spray paints or toxic adhesives are used.

- Make certain your work chair is comfortable and of the proper height. An adjustable, rolling, swivel chair is convenient for swift ergonomic movement.

Having a cluttered or disorganized stained-glass or mosaic space is not only inefficient but also can be potentially very dangerous. Broken glass or other sharp materials present cutting hazards. It is also very helpful to have a well-organized area so you can create when inspiration strikes.

Stained Glass and Mosaics

2

Things to Consider

- Is your stained-glass or mosaic crafting area potentially dangerous due to sharp pieces being improperly stored?

- Is it difficult to reach your adhesives, grouting materials, and certain tools when you need them due to their inconvenient positioning in your space?

- Do you often find yourself wasting time searching for a particular color of glass or tile that you know you have but just can't find?

- Is too little space a primary contributor to an ill-functioning work area?

- Do you find that you don't accomplish as much as you would like to because much of your work time is spent cleaning up after yourself?

One of the most important elements in a stained-glass or mosaic work space is having an area large enough to spread out tools and supplies. If you do not already have a large desk or table, this is a wise investment.

Keeping toxic or potentially hazardous products in a safe place is imperative in this type of craft space. Flux, patina, adhesives, etching creams, and finishing compound should be stored out of reach of children and pets, or locked up if necessary, as shown at left.

If possible, keep your glass grinder, or grozing stone, on your worktable in an area that is out of the way yet still reachable. Since this is a tool that will be used fairly frequently, you will want to be able to reach it with minimal effort.

Other commonly used tools and materials should be stored on your work surface and organized according to size, shape, or order of use. For example, glass cutters, circle/strip cutters, fids, lead dykes, and notching tools can be stored together in glass jars or terra-cotta pots, while glass-cutting oils fit conveniently into small boxes or decorative tins.

(Opposite) Store heavier items along the bottom shelf to avoid back strain, and keep those things that you rarely use in bins along the top shelf. Grouping like items in specific sections of a shelving unit makes it convenient to find exactly what you are looking for.

A pegboard with multiple hooks is a great idea for a stained-glass work space. Copper foil, solder, hacksaws, shears, and stained-glass hammers can all be stored neatly on a pegboard according to size, shape, or function.

Glass storage, of course, is another thing to consider when planning a stained-glass work space. Separate your glass into categories that work well for you. For example, you may want to separate glass by color, texture, then opacity, or by texture, opacity, then color. Having specific areas along your shelves dedicated to a particular type of glass will make it easy to find what you are looking for quickly and efficiently. Once larger pieces of glass have been cut, you may want to save scraps for future projects. Purchasing containers in which to hold glass scraps will keep them neatly contained, yet still accessible.

Be certain to clean your work surface often when using it. Glass shavings and shards left on the table can scratch the glass you are working with and cut your fingers. Keep a bench brush, dustpan, and garbage can lined with a paper bag near your work space for easy disposal.

A mosaic work space will likely be filled with a variety of tools and supplies. I find it is best to keep my tools separated by use: drawing and design tools, surface preparation tools, cutting tools, attaching tools, grouting tools, and finishing tools are all kept together in designated containers. This makes it very convenient to find exactly what I am looking for simply by reading the labels on the outside of each box.

Because mosaic tesserae come in various sizes, it is a good idea to keep them separated by size, color, and type. For example, keep smalti, tile, stone, stained glass, and china pieces in designated positions on your shelf space, separated by size and color.

(Opposite top) One creative idea for this type of work space is to mosaic a label onto a decorative ribbon or directly onto the container for quick identification.

(Opposite right) Labeling the outside of storage containers is imperative for finding things quickly and easily. Print out a list of titles for each container, and cut them into tags. Tags can be tied with a cute ribbon to wire baskets, or glued to thin magnets for securing to metal boxes.

(This page) These shallow drawers are perfect for separating glass and tesserae according to size or color. The drawer fronts already have a space to insert labels, so simply typing or handwriting them is the only task remaining.

61

(This page) This magnetic board is not only a decorative accent piece, it is a reliable method for keeping small, easily lost pieces together and out of children's reach. Each of the small containers has a tight-fitting lid to ensure nothing will fall out of the tins, while a sturdy magnet has been secured to the back. Although a board like this can be purchased, get creative and make your own! It will match the decor of your own craft area while allowing you to demonstrate your abilities.

Other Ideas

(Left) Mosaic artist Gina Galichia suggests that when you see a container that you are drawn to but have no immediate use for, purchase it anyway. It's likely you will be able to incorporate it into your space at some point, especially if the item has many small compartments for separating tesserae, such as a vintage cash register, muffin tins, or silverware boxes.

(Right and below) Pretty wicker baskets in a neutral color are complementary to the natural shells and sea stars inside, while clear glass jars make it easy to see the tesserae within.

Guest Artist:
Linda Woodward

Although Linda Woodward's stained-glass work space is very small, she likes to keep things well organized. Organization, she says "is very important to me. One thing that helps me is an old department store display cabinet with glass drawer fronts."

The comfortable chairs along one wall do not take up an excessive amount of space, but still provide a suitable area for visitor's to observe while Linda works. The wide countertops that line two of the walls present ample room for working comfortably. The cabinets beneath are perfect for storing the many tools and supplies used in stained-glass projects.

65

Stenciling and rubber stamping involve a great deal of small, easily misplaced materials. Creating a system that makes sense to you is imperative to keeping order in your creative space.

Stamps and Stencils

Because stamps and stencils are the main element for your particular craft, it is likely you have an abundance of them. Grouping them may seem intimidating at first; however, figuring out the best way to organize stamps and stencils is the first step in maintaining a smooth-running work area.

Decide whether you will organize alphabetically or by subject. Grouping stamps that depict characters that begin with "A" is an excellent and easy way to get started. However, it might make more sense for you to place all of your animal stamps or stencils in one drawer, with birds, jungle animals, or fish grouped in separate partitions. Your occasion stamps and stencils, such as Christmas, graduation, or birthday, can be kept in another drawer or area.

Ink Pads

To avoid having stray ink unintentionally leak onto a project, try keeping all of your ink pads in the top few drawers near your work space. This will keep the ink close at hand, but you will rarely have to remove ink pads from the drawer while you work. Line each drawer with contact paper to prevent any ink spills or leaks from damaging your furniture.

Another alternative is to purchase wire racks to set your ink pads on. Make certain there is enough room to flip open the lids, and that you purchase large enough racks to accommodate several colors.

Scissors, Adhesives, Stickers, and Other Supplies

Remember to keep any supplies that are used frequently within reach on your work surface. Those items that are not used often can be stored in drawers, bins, or closets. However, make certain to keep a good inventory of supplies stored out-of-sight. Oftentime, when hidden from view, ink will dry out, rendering it unusable. Having too many unseen supplies can result in buying multiples of the same item.

(Left) Having a shelf conveniently placed over your workstation is great—you rarely have to leave to look for favorite stamps or often-used ink colors, resulting in less distraction.

(Above) Hanging dowels or other slim rods can make spotting and accessing stickers a snap.

Guest Artist: Suze Weinberg

Suze's creative space functions very well thanks to a plethora of clearly labeled sliding wire baskets. All of her supplies are at hand when she needs them, and her work area remains organized because she puts everything away as soon as she is finished with it.

As you can see from the photograh on pages 66–67, Suze keeps the items she uses most often, in her immediate work area. The melting pots are always filled with ultrathick embossing enamel to ensure efficient work time. All of her other items are stored behind her in the wire-basket system.

Although Suze says she would like to have a slightly wider space along with "a really good deep closet," she has effectively created a work space that accommodates her supplies and allows her to create with few distractions.

(Above left and opposite) Rubber-stamping artist Suze Weinberg recommends decorating your creative space with your own handiwork as it "reaffirms your talent, makes you feel proud of what you've made, and keeps you inspired."

(Left) Clearly labeled, the abundance of sliding-wire basket drawers make it easy to see what Suze has on-hand, as well as to locate the desired supplies within seconds.

Guest Artist: Dee Gruenig

Dee Gruenig's work space is a sanctuary of organization. In fact, Dee doesn't even use any of her tools and supplies until they have been organized in a well-functioning manner and stored in a container that is absolutely perfect for that particular item.

Dee's favorite type of container for tools and supplies are clear, white, or black plastic containers. She livens up their neutral bases by attaching handmade labels flourished in bright colors. The drawers surrounding her desk are filled only with supplies she needs on hand, such as her pens and stamps. Papers and other supplies are kept in drawers, arranged and categorized according to frequency of use.

Storing her 5,000-plus rubbe stamps isn't a problem with the customized system she has created for herself. Dee categorizes her stamps according to theme, and keeps only those she uses most often in her studio. After determining groups for her rubber stamps, Dee creates an arrangement for the stamps to fit into an 11"x17" tray, and makes an imprint of each stamp on an acrylic placemat. She then makes a photocopy of the arrangement, laminates it, and lines the inside of a box frame. This gives each stamp a permanent home, so that Dee always knows where to put it when she is finished

(Above) This comfortable chair allows for hours of creation, while Dee's most frequently used pens are so conveniently located, she never wastes time hunting them down.

(Opposite) This is another workstation in Dee's space, also set up for maximum efficiency. When you love to organize as much as Dee does, you're bound to have everything you need within reach.

using it. Each of these trays is labeled according to category, and placed along runners to create personalized drawers.

As Dee can't fit all of the stamps in her small studio, she is constantly reevaluating which ones are used most often. Those that are not used on a regular basis are delegated to shallow, rectangular boxes, which are then lined, labeled, and stored in the garage. This system makes it very easy for Dee to find the desired stamp when she does need to use it.

Special pens play a major role in Dee's artistic creations. It is imperative that she has a range of options because of her technique of applying various colors onto each stamp before inscribing. Because Dee could not find the perfect storage unit that would also keep her pens right at her fingertips, she decided to create her own by hot-gluing the pen caps onto a holder. This way, Dee can grab whatever color pen she needs at the moment, and never have to worry about misplacing the cap. Pens of secondary importance are kept in a second container near her work surface.

Though her space is small, Dee places a priority on using just the right item for the job—and that includes furniture. She keeps three chairs in her work space for varying activities. Two chairs are for sitting at her desk and other work areas, while the third is meant solely for reading and relaxing.

(Above) Dee's labeled boxes look great in her space due to their coordination with the rest of the decor while functioning as an efficient means of categorizing and storing smaller items. The laminated drawer inserts ensure an ever-accurate system of organization, while the labels on the outside of the shallow drawers reduce time spent hunting for a specific item.

(Opposite) Dee has three different work spaces where she can sit down. This desk has convenient plastic bins along the wall so she can easily access a specific file without looking through an abundance of files.

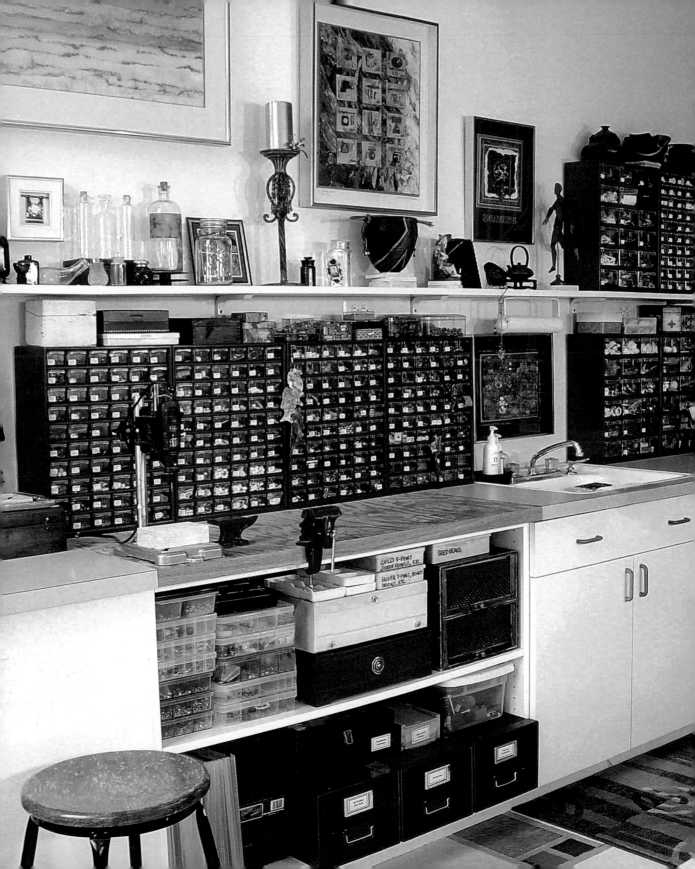

Guest Artist: Susan Pickering Rothamel

Susan Pickering Rothamel's creative space is an organized haven of creativity. By grouping like objects together, Susan can always find what she is looking for while keeping continuity in studio design by employing portable, sturdy white or transparent containers. Susan also uses an old enamel tray that holds small items and disposable condiment cups filled with liquid supplies such as adhesives. The condiment cups help her to avoid extensive cleanup, as she can throw them out when they are empty, while the tray enables her to easily transport supplies around her space. Another aspect of Susan's space that works well for her is having portions of the room designated to a specific task, such as framing, claywork, textiles, papers arts, or even paperwork.

(Opposite and above) Susan says, "Since I use such a broad range of materials in my work, keeping it tidy is imperative. I learned early on that when my work space is messy or disheveled, either too much time is spent searching for things or it becomes 'an accident waiting to happen' ... usually onto the art itself!"

(Above) Clear storage containers alongside Susan's work space make it easy to find what she needs without looking through multiple cabinets and drawers. Bins, boxes, baskets, or tins that are not transparent are always clearly labeled.

(Left) Susan recommends not storing items more than one layer deep as they tend to get lost or dry out from nonuse.

(Above right) Areas that are too small for creating large projects can oftentimes be utilized as extra storage space. Here, small bookshelves house objects that can be stored out of the way, but still close enough to provide inspiration.

(Right) The business side of Susan's art is housed inside her studio; however, it remains an independent portion of the space.

The art of scrapbook making can range from very simple to intricately detailed. Regardless of your style, scrapbook creation requires a multitude of tools and materials. Many of these tools and materials are very small or oddly shaped, creating housing dilemmas. This chapter will teach you to organize the area in which you scrapbook, so that all of your tools and materials are easily accessible yet efficiently stored.

- Do you have so much paper that it is difficult to find the particular color, pattern, or texture you are looking for?

- Do you oftentimes have a particular photograph in mind for a scrapbook page, but simply cannot find it amidst all the other photographs you have?

- Do you have a hard time finding smaller items, such as stickers, paper punches, scissors, and adhesives?

- Are your often-used materials, such as a paper cutter stored beneath other supplies, making it difficult to access?

- Have you ever visited the scrapbook supply store and returned home to find that you have purchased the same patterned paper that you already have in stock?

(Above) The ample work surface in this scrapbooking space accommodates a computer for archiving photos and special pages; a supply stand for pens, adhesives, and cutting tools; and still has room to spare for spreading out projects while working.

(Opposite) This well-stocked armoire contains an abundance of paper, cardstock, and decorative boxes for various tools and supplies. The small television also provides entertainment for especially lengthy scrapbooking sessions.

Visualize your most-frequently visited scrapbook store. Although there are many reasons to visit a particular store—proximity to your home, price, selection—one reason is that you can always find exactly what you're looking for with minimal hassle. Ask yourself what it is you like about their setup, and see if you can figure out ways to emulate that in your own space. Begin by breaking down your tools and materials into categories.

Papers and Cardstocks

Chances are, various papers and cardstocks are your most-often-used materials. As most scrapbookers keep a large supply of these items on hand, it can be one of the most difficult issues for organization.

Begin by deciding where you will store your papers. Standard 8½"x11" and 12"-square stackable paper trays can be purchased online or in a scrapbook supply store, which easily takes care of storage issues.

Shelves work well if you would like to see your paper on display. A unit with several different compartments is a good system and allows for distinct separation. Building a shelving unit from plywood is both simple and cost-effective. If you aren't comfortable sawing and hammering the wood to your specifications, set the plywood on top of cinderblocks, filing cabinets, or

stackable plastic storage bins with drawers. This will easily allow you to create your desired shelf height, while allowing plenty of room for assorted papers and cardstocks on each shelf.

If your craft area cannot accommodate any new furniture, use existing drawers to stack papers and cardstocks inside. You can buy or create dividers to separate various types of paper. Adhere small swatches of paper to the dividers to distinguish between varieties at a glance. It might also prove useful to record other information on the dividers, such as the color name, the manufacturer's name, or the SKU number.

To begin grouping various types of paper, lay out your entire stock on the floor or a table. One way to categorize is by separating the cardstocks from the papers, then dividing by size. Separate solid colors from patterns, and patterns into subcategories such as Christmas, birthday, stripes, or plaids. Specialty handcrafted papers or those with texture also can be placed in their own categories.

Now, arrange the papers and cardstocks in the stackable trays, shelves, or drawers, so that each category is distinguishable as well as clearly labeled if necessary.

Adhesives and Removers

Some of your more-frequently used supplies, adhesives, and removers should be stored on your desk or work surface if possible. Purchasing a wire basket or wooden box large enough to house all of these items together will keep them neatly contained yet still within your reach.

Scissors

Decorative-edged and regular craft scissors are also used often enough that they should be stored in your immediate work area. Purchase a container large enough to keep all of your scissors together. If you also use a paper cutter, try to place it on

(Opposite and this page) Paper can be stored in so many different ways. Shallow drawers can accommodate a great deal of paper, which can then be organized by size, color, texture, or any other means that works well for you and your space. Shelves are also a great way to keep paper separated as you can simply scan the storage area to quickly find exactly what you need.

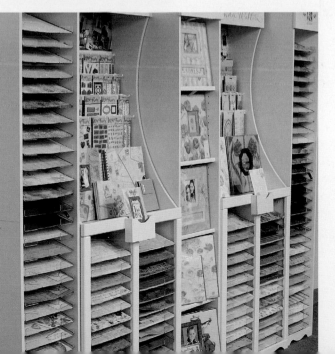

your work surface or in the immediate vicinity to prevent unnecessary trips for cutting.

Other Supplies

Scrapbooking is an art that is constantly changing. There are so many diverse ways of creating a scrapbook, that you probably have various supplies such as photo corners, stencils, or diecuts. Those items that you use most often should be placed on the work surface or within easy reach, while less-frequently used supplies can be stored in closets, drawers, or cabinets. Remember, there are so many storage options available that you can be just as creative in your organization as when you create a beautiful scrapbook.

(Left) If you are a traditionalist who loves using film as opposed to digital images, keep photos archived in beautiful albums. Images can be categorized by date, event, or people involved.

(Top) Sometimes storing beautiful items in the open can be aesthetically pleasing. Vintage frames such as these can also be used to display scrapbook pages as art as opposed to keeping them confined to the pages of a book.

(Above) Storing smaller supplies in decorative bottles is a great way to keep your space aesthetic yet functional. The labels here have been made from vintage postcards, adding a touch of nostalgia to an effective means of organization.

(Opposite) This intricate shelving unit provides a vast amount of space for keeping a range of tools and materials. Drawers, shelves, and decorative boxes are great places in which to store photos, scissors, adhesives, and embellishments.

Other Ideas

(This page) Whether your scrapbooking area is large or small, finding cost-effective ways of storing items can be as simple as visiting a flea market or yard sale. Old cigar boxes can hold pencils, scissors, adhesives, or any other item while adding a touch of vintage charm to the room. An old top hat makes a wonderful space to store ephemera, while stocking the shelves with aged books can provide inspiration for making altered scrapbooks.

(Opposite) Inspiration can be fleeting; however, this problem can be easily fixed by surrounding yourself with a plethora of interesting pictures and found objects. This space is filled with items that work well as decorative pieces, but that can also be easily incorporated into a project at a moment's notice.

Guest Artist:
Sandi Genovese

Sandi's creative space is so small that a great organizational system is imperative. One trick Sandi has employed is using a rolling filing cabinet. The drawers add storage space for rubber stamps, ink pads, and other tools, while the top functions as a work space as shown at left.

The end tables in Sandi's space are actually wicker baskets that hold her paper cutter and adhesive machine, while built-in shelves are great for storing sticker rolls and die-cutting equipment. The extra bathroom has also been converted into work space, with book shelves hiding the shower while adding even more storage. Sandi has lined one wall of her space with stacking plastic drawers that allow her to see all of the contents inside. She says, "These handy drawers hold nearly all of my craft embellishments, from ribbons and fibers to paint and ink pads, to metal words, charms, wires, and everything in between." Sandi even converted a closet into her office space, having a desk made to fit inside. The shelves hold boxes and baskets that contain office and art supplies as well as photos. She also keeps a rolling file beneath the desk, where items are filed by theme as shown on opposite page.

Paper crafting involves a vast array of materials depending on your particular style. Three-dimensional paper crafts are boxes, baskets, bottles, or any number of items embellished with paper and turned into art. Flat paper crafting projects also utilize an abundance of fun and unique objects. However, given the endless options available for paper crafts, it can be overwhelming to find space to not only house your supplies but also keep them orderly.

Closet Organizers

For many of us, a small space is a huge problem in crafting. Personally, my paper-crafting room doubles as a guest bedroom, so it is imperative that I keep the room orderly for my frequent houseguests. By purchasing a large canvas closet organizer, I have created an abundance of storage in a fairly compact space. Canvas closet organizers provide endless options, because each piece can be purchased separately to accommodate any particular space.

An over-the-door hanging organizer is a great addition to any closet. The hooks fit neatly over the door, so there is no need to create holes in the wood for nails or screws. One great way to arrange this type of organizer is alphabetically. After determining which items will be stored here, print or handwrite labels to attach to each pocket. You can then arrange by letter so you will always know exactly where to look for a certain item. Alternatives to alphabetizing the door organizer are to store by weight or frequency of use. Heavier items should be stored along the bottom, while scissors, adhesives, and other supplies used daily should be kept at eye level.

(Left) The beautifully embellished closet doors in this paper-crafting/guest bedroom give the space a warm, homey feel, while the hanging doorknob embellishments provide a feng shui approach for good flow.

(Opposite) Once opened, a plethora of paper-crafting materials are revealed. Despite being well stocked, the closet remains neatly organized.

Several of the in-closet organizer compartments can be used to store papers according to size, texture, or color. Larger paper can be placed on overhead shelves, or stored inside an attractive vintage suitcase to keep everything looking tidy. Smaller scraps can be separated according to theme or the type of project in which the paper was last used, and stored in pull-out drawers.

Smaller items, such as photo corners, charms, beads, or buttons, can also be stored in creative containers on designated shelves within the closet organizer. Using cute paper-crafted tags is a great way to label jars and drawers while illustrating your talents in the art of paper crafting.

(This page) Individual compartments can be designated to hold just about anything you like. From utilitarian photo corners to inspirational paper projects, these organizers are the perfect solution for any crafter's space.

(Opposite) The over-the-door canvas organizer adds even more storage to the closet. Because it is flat, it does not create excess bulk, preventing the doors from being shut. However, the many pockets ensure plenty of storage for so many small tools and embellishments.

Shelves

If your craft space doesn't have a closet, shelves are always a great backup for creating the space you need within the room. Purchasing a large bookcase, cabinet, or simply attaching some shelves to the wall can create vast amounts of space.

Personally, I like to use stylishly embellished boxes to keep my shelves looking tidy. Boxes with lids are neatly labeled on the outside so that I always know exactly where to find what I am looking for. I also use vertical magazine boxes to keep various papers in an easy-to-access, categorized order.

(Opposite) From far away, you can see there are many boxes, binders, and books stored on the shelves of this closet. However, the arrangement keeps them looking nice as well as functional due to a well-thought-out system.

(This page) These charming handwritten tags identify exactly what is stored within each of the boxes. This way, a lengthy search is never required to find something in particular.

Armoire

An armoire is a beautiful decorative piece for any guest or crafting room, providing plenty of storage. If you like to watch television while you are working, a set fits neatly inside, yet will remain hidden from view once the armoire doors are closed.

The shelves in a piece of furniture this size are generally very deep, and are a great place to keep over-sized papers. Longer boxes filled with decorative-edged scissors, adhesives, or ribbon can be kept here as well, then pulled out and placed near your work surface only when being used.

Work Surface

A large desk or table is ideal for a paper-crafting work space, as multiple items are oftentimes used simultaneously, creating the need for a larger surface. However, this isn't always a possibility, especially if your craft area doubles as a bedroom or living space. If this is the case, a small desk will suffice as long as your materials can be placed within reach without impeding on your elbow room. Purchase a small rolling cart, if possible, to make your materials mobile while adding a bit of extra storage.

(Above) An armoire with extra shelves and a television add storage and a little entertainment for those days when a little "company" is desired during paper-crafting time.

(Opposite) The work surface is placed conveniently at the foot of the bed. Although this desk is somewhat small, all of the wonderful shelves and storage in the room make it easy to put things away and keep the desk uncluttered.

(Opposite) Anna's light and airy space is ideal for creation. This large worktable provides her with enough room to spread out her current projects without having to worry about overlapping piles. The large window brings in a great view—perfect for inspiration any time it's needed.

(Above) This small rolling cart is convenient for traveling around the room. Because Anna has so many work surfaces, the mobility makes it easy to have all of her supplies at her fingertips no matter where she happens to be working.

Guest Artist: Anna Corba

When it comes to Anna Corba's creative space, her main goal is to keep as many materials available as possible without having them overflow into the actual working areas. Looking around her studio, she says, is all she needs to keep herself motivated. If that fails, she just opens a drawer and starts shuffling through its contents until another piece begins to invent itself. "Wanting to get my hands on and make use of what I have collected is infinitely stimulating and fun," she says.

Anna enjoys working in an uncluttered space, so her work area contains several tables. Either end of a particular table contains a basket of often-used materials—glue sticks, various scissors, photo corners, pencils, black ink pads. This gives her easy access to basic supplies.

Tables are placed according to where they fit and what window view Anna wants to take advantage of. There is "more of a creative dance to the way I move among areas as opposed to a logical, regimented structure," Anna says. In general, she tries to use one table as a desk, one for beginning projects, and another for finishing projects. She also has a table for overflow or future projects that she just can't get into yet. This table can become quite layered with odds and ends, and serves as a general inspiration area when her creativity needs some stimulation.

Bulletin boards are an important source of organization and inspiration. Anna keeps one for visual stimulation; one for invitations, thank-you notes, and upcoming events; and one another for quotes and other literary material.

For organizing paper, Anna has two large antique map drawer cabinets. She organizes the papers according to type: tissue, decorative, thick, thin, single pieces, notepads, etc., and she labels each drawer on the outside. In addition to the drawers, she has quite a few stacking boxes that are also labeled on the outside. She organizes these according to color—blue/green, black, brown, red, etc. She also organizes the boxes according to types of ephemera, from photos to old letters to images. This keeps her collections from becoming overwhelming and she can check easily to see what category may be low when she is on her way to a show.

Anna is a big fan of sets of drawers. Along with using them for paper, she fills them with her rubber stamps and ink pads, once again labeled according to general category on the outside of each drawer.

(Above) This antique memo holder is perfect for displaying important business cards, friendly postcards, or any special piece that Anna would like to show.

Tip:

A small tiered cake stand is a great way to keep items in view, without having to stack them on top of one another. The array of containers used to hold embellishments adds to the room with a touch of vintage charm.

A firm believer in having zillions of interesting containers to hold all her objects, Anna provides fabulous homes for everything from simple tape to vintage buttons. Anna loves using vintage wire baskets, pretty boxes, sundae glasses, muffin tins, old bread pans, cake stands, glass milk jars, and more. Anna says, "You'd think I cook, but I don't—I guess my studio is the ultimate pastry shop in disguise!" Open shelves are lined with containers filled with buttons, beads, and other materials. They are always easy to see and grab.

On Anna's finishing table are quite a few wire baskets and three-tiered cake stands that hold ribbon. This is practical because it provides easy access, but it's also visually inspiring. She keeps close by the colors and textures that she loves the most. "This way," she says, "just sitting down at the table to get started is a feast for the eye and food for the soul!"

(Right) Rulers are not just for measuring in Anna's space. Often incorporated into art pieces, this collection stands close at hand for any project. Other tools also inhabit the ceramic jar, making it convenient to reach for whatever is needed.

(Left) Anna is lucky to have an abundance of shelves for storing supplies. However, she keeps them tidy by grouping like objects, and storing smaller pieces in designated containers.

(Below) Old books offer so many options for paper crafts, Anna keeps her studio well stocked. This cute wicker basket displays a few of the titles waiting to be added to a wonderful project.

Tip:

Anna says, "I organize my ephemera according to color—blue/green, black, brown, reds; or by theme—birds, French, etc. This keeps my collections from becoming too overwhelming, and I can check easily when I am on my way to buy at a trade show."

(This page) Small drawers are perfect for storing away bits of ephemera. Adding a few coats of paint and some embellishments gives them personality, making your space exactly that—yours.

(Opposite) Anna has turned this entire wall into a bulletin board. It's great for posting reminders, inspirational photos, or anything else she loves to look at.

The materials used in a beading work area can often-times be condensed into a fairly small amount of space. However, because so many supplies are used, it can be difficult to maintain order amidst the several minuscule pieces.

Your work surface should be completely level so that beads won't roll onto the floor, resulting in tiresome retrieval. If you have the space and are able, purchase a large enough desk or table that all of your supplies can be stored at hand. Even a system as simple as filling some charming ceramic jars with beading materials can be helpful.

Beads

There are so many types of beads available that it is imperative to arrange them in a way that makes sense for your particular work space. Choosing a means of storage is the first step in organizing your beads. Purchasing a multicompartment container with small drawers is a great idea for separating beads. If the thought of a large plastic storage container in your space is less than appealing to you, you could purchase compartmentalized trays to place inside the drawers of a beautiful antique dresser. Beads can also be separated and kept in glass bottles, ceramic jars, or embellished tins.

(Left) Compartmentalized drawers keep beads, wire cutters, clasps, findings, and just about anything neatly contained and tucked away.

(Opposite) A small cloth or pad is helpful when working on a surface such as this smooth desk. The beads will not roll too far from your project, while the various containers are within reach to put away extras.

When undertaking bead reorganization, you should place a small label inside of each compartment with the brand, store name where the beads were purchased, restock number, and color name so that beads can be restocked with minimal hassle. Handwritten labels can look very charming if done neatly; however, if your penmanship leaves something to be desired, typing identification labels is wise.

Separate your beads into specific categories, such as seed, bugle, glass, crystal, bone, ceramic, clay, metal, shell, wood, and plastic. Subcategorize by size, color, and finish. Place each type of bead into its designated compartment or container, making certain that those beads used most often are the ones closest to your immediate work area.

(Top right) The beads you use most often should be kept right on your work surface, in close reach. These decorative ceramic jars hold a great number of beads for very large projects.

(Right) These glass jars make a great place to store smaller objects. Their vintage appearance matches the color scheme of the room while still allowing the crafter to see the contents within.

(Opposite) Although these wooden drawer sets are very small, they can still hold a great amount of beading materials. The felt-lined drawers provide soft cushioning for more fragile objects.

(Right) Being organized does not necessarily mean things have to look boring. This drawer is specifically set aside for extra packages of beads that have not yet been opened. The cute but simple ties atop each bundle keep the packages sorted by size, type of bead, and color.

(Below) This beaded basket adds a personal touch to the room, while keeping the items in use at hand. The container can be easily stored away in a drawer when beading is not in progress, in order to keep the desktop free and clear.

Tip:

Your beading area may become a repository for possessions that don't really belong there, whether they belong to you or a family member. If this is the case, designate an empty bin or basket for stray items. Pick a specific day each week to put stray items away yourself, or assign a family member to do it.

Clasps and Findings

Clasps and findings are also pieces that tend to get misplaced in an unorganized space. Much like your actual beads, these items can also be separated into categories and placed into compartments.

Wire

Depending on the projects you choose to make, you may have multiple kinds and gauges of wire at your disposal. However, keeping all of your wire organized can be taxing. Decorative baskets can be used to store wire which has been separated by type or gauge. These are also a good option for smaller spaces, because baskets can be placed directly on the floor.

(Above) Keeping clasps and findings in specific compartments in your storage unit is a great way to organize them when not in use. However, when you are sitting at your work surface, keep small jewelry pieces set aside on cute plates within reach. Once finished, simply pour the contents of each saucer into the designated storage compartment.

(Right) Beading requires a multitude of wires for stringing beads. This antique box keeps spools compact and portable, while maintaining aesthetic appeal.

As wire generally is sold on a spool, it can also be stored in a storage container made specifically for thread, which can generally be purchased in your local craft store.

Always make certain each spool of wire is clearly marked with the gauge. This makes it very simple to reach for the proper size when needed, as well as to know what needs replacing when you have a trip to the craft store planned.

Even extra bits of wire are worth saving. You might need just a tiny bit for a future project. These bits of wire or string can be kept in separate compartments in your bead storage unit, or pinned to a bulletin board for easy retrieval.

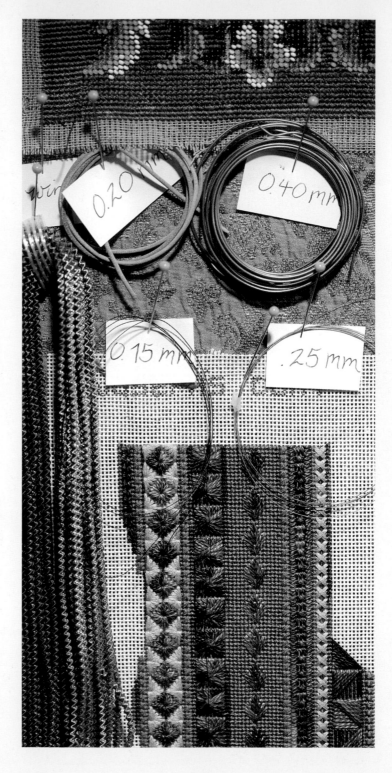

(Right) Bulletin boards function as more than just an area to display favorite photos and reminders. Extra bits of wire can be pinned the board for future use, along with a note to remind you of the wire's gauge.

Tools

Wire cutters, needle-nosed pliers, crimping pliers, and round-nosed pliers should all be stored together. They can be placed neatly into a decorated terra-cotta pot, lined up neatly on shelves, or hung on a pegboard labeled with the name of each tool.

(Left) The ceramic jars, also shown on page 114, provide additional storage for smaller tools.

(Above) This terra-cotta pot is small enough to allow you to find what you need without being overwhelming. The light glaze provides a soft touch, adding to the overall color scheme of the room.

Making the Most of a Small Space

If your workroom is quite small, adding a few decorative mirrors will be incredibly beneficial. Reflecting natural light from the window, the space will appear much larger, while adding a venue for inspirational items. These mirrors not only add personality to the room but they also act as a bulletin board, filled with photos of family and friends.

Other Ideas

(This page) Adding your own vintage-style labels personalizes inexpensive glass jars; distressing the lids gives a nostalgic feel to your space.

If you don't already have an area set aside for your craft, take the time to create some space. When you organize your projects and keep your materials at your finger-tips, you'll find that you are more likely to stay motivated to work on current projects, and more inspired to begin new ones.

Things to Consider

- Do you have a specific work space set aside for your yarn craft or needlework, or do you work in a common area such as the living room?

- Do your materials from separate projects get mixed up together?

- Do you tuck projects away and find it difficult to stay motivated enough to return to old projects?

- Are old patterns that have gone completely out of style still mixed in with new ones?

- Do you have to get up to find a pair of scissors or a crochet hook when working?

Yarn crafts and needlework involve more tools than many people think. Aside from yarn and floss, other accessories like needles, hooks, scissors, row counters, ring markers, and yarn winders all need a designated home in your work space.

Work Space and Storage

The size of your work area will, of course, depend on how many materials you have on hand. A few shelves may be enough for some, while others may need several shelves, drawers, and possibly a closet.

Be certain to designate a portion of your craft area to store your current projects when you're not working on them. When you have a home for projects, you will be less likely to lose them or forget how many projects you have begun. You can keep each project, with all the necessary materials, in its own basket for transporting around the home. A sealed bag helps to keep all the materials together when taking the project outside your home.

Fibers and Fabrics

Yarn storage is the first thing to consider when organizing a knitting or crochet area. Determine the categories you would like to separate the yarn into—color, texture, or weight. Shallow drawers allow you to store skeins in a single layer so that you can see them all at once.

A hanging shoe organizer works well, too. Just hang the organizer from a closet rod and stack it with multiple skeins. Canvas organizers are a good choice because they allow you to sew deep pockets on the sides for storing needles.

Organize embroidery flosses and ribbons by color and store them in single layers in shallow drawers. Clear plastic drawers allow you to access the right color quickly and easily.

Keeping extra Aida fabric, even-weave, cotton, linen, and other fabrics together in your craft space allows you to pick out the correct material for the job without spending time searching. Roll similar fabrics together, tie in a pretty bow, and store in a single layer in a shallow drawer or box. This allows you to store more fabrics—while keeping them free of creases—and to see your entire supply at a single glance.

Patterns

Both yarn crafts and needlework require charts and patterns, items

(Opposite) A large work surface provides plenty of room for all your tools and materials as well as space for creating the project at hand.

(Top left) Rolling your canvas squares is a great way to keep them clean and wrinkle-free. The ribbon ties can be used as a color code for sorting your collection.

(Left) A cigar box filled with floss keeps the colors for your current project close by, without risking the skeins getting tangled up on a messy desktop.

125

that can stack up and get disorganized before you know it. Before you begin organizing your patterns, gather every sheet you own and sort through them to determine which are dated and which you would like to keep on hand. Then you can begin to separate them by type: sweaters, afghans, floral, holiday, etc.

Store each category of patterns in its own drawer and label it on the outside for quick reference. A second option is to keep patterns in labeled binders. Place them in clear page protectors so that often-used pages will last longer. Whenever you add a new page to your collection, take a few minutes to sort through the rest and discard any you no longer need. That way your patterns will always stay current and you won't become overwhelmed by excess papers.

Tools, Embellishments, and More

Crochet hooks, knitting needles, and embroidery needles can be stored in shallow boxes or in drawers. Use a drawer organizer made for pencils and pens to separate the tools by size or gauge, then label the box or drawer on the outside for quick and easy access. Store some embroidery needles in a decorative pincushion and place it on a desk or shelf for quick access.

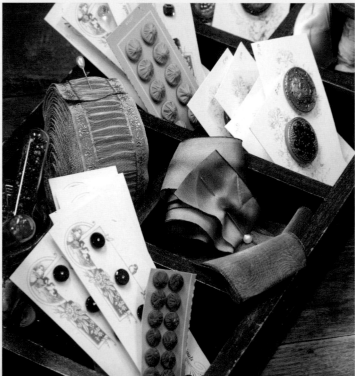

Drawer organizers with different-sized compartments can also be used to house scissors, row counters, ring markers, and other helpful tools. Think of other nontraditional uses for office supplies. Use a rolodex to catalogue dye formulas or the amount of yarn needed for certain projects. You can use the back of the card for recording personal notes and information such as, "Summer Blue yarn was used on Sara's Christmas present in 2005."

Find space for larger tools that do not fit as easily in shallow drawers. Embroidery hoops can be hung on the wall on ornamental hooks. Keep your swift or yarn winder clamped to a desk or table in your work space, or keep it in its own cubbyhole on a shelf.

Be certain to make space for all your little extras, like buttons, beads, and other embellishments. Buttons look pretty and are easy to find when placed together in clear containers. Beads can be arranged by size, color, material, etc., in clear drawers with several small compartments, or in small glass jars or containers.

(Top opposite) Drawer pulls are an excellent place to attach labels. You will know right away what is stored within.

(Bottom opposite) Buttons attached to cards and sorted by similar styles makes it a snap to find the right color, size, or look for the project at hand. You can simply cut off those needed without worrying about misplacing the others.

(This page) Keeping beads in small containers within a larger jar creates a visually appealing storage solution.

(This page and opposite) Containers can be a needle crafter's best friend. From wicker baskets to modern metal tins, portable storage makes it easy to craft where you please, while allowing you to maintain style in your space. However, the minimalist approach works, too.

Quilting work spaces can be difficult to organize, especially if you don't have a lot of space. Even if you do have more room, keeping your sewing area free of scraps and other debris can take more time and effort than you are willing to give. However, finding an organizational system that works in your particular space is the first step in creating the best quilts possible.

Things to Consider

- Is your quilting space so small that you oftentimes feel overwhelmed by too many items?

- Are your storage areas so cluttered with tools and materials that you have trouble finding items?

- Are scraps, squares, and large fabric pieces all stored in the same place, causing difficulty in finding the correct size?

- Does your thread get tangled up together due to a lack of organization?

- Do you have a difficult time finding the pattern you are looking for because they are shoved into a drawer with little organization?

Guest Artist: Freddy Moran

Freddy Moran's creative space is as inspiring as it is colorful. She keeps it functioning through a wonderful organizational system that involves a rolling table, plenty of open shelves, and multiple sewing stations for days in which friends join her in her quilting. A sliding wall creates extra storage, while a neat reading corner with a comfortable chair offers a quiet space for a short rest.

There are several options available for getting the most out of a limited area. A shelving unit to accommodate several yards of fabric is imperative to a well-functioning space. Cubbies can often work even better than shelves and can be purchased in many furniture or online

(Left) The wire bins and drawers of the rolling table add storage for items that need to be mobile. The countertop adds a good-size work space for laying out cloth to be cut in various shapes.

(Opposite) Having a countertop installed along the length of the wall is a wonderful idea for having extra work space. Not only can Freddy fit two sewing machines in her craft room, she also has room to design.

stores. If you do not like the idea of open shelves or cubbies, consider purchasing a vintage armoire at a second-hand store and refinishing it to your liking. Once you have a means of storage available, categorize your fabrics by solid color and pattern. Roll larger pieces of fabric into cylindrical shapes or rectangles and stack fabric, packing tightly in place. Purchase several stacking wire baskets or small wicker baskets to store various sizes and colors of small fabric pieces and scraps. By using stacking wire baskets, you save space by storing your items vertically, while wicker baskets can easily slide beneath your cutting table.

A great way to make an inexpensive cutting surface is to purchase several cabinets of the desired height. Simply drill a piece of plywood, finished to your liking, to the cabinets to create a table with custom storage. In spaces where having a permanent cutting table is not possible, purchase a folding table that can be easily taken down and

(Top right) Even small scraps can be used on future projects. Designate a scrap drawer for holding various-sized pieces of fabric that could potentially work as a component of another quilt.

(Right) Freddy suggests having a floor that is easy to sweep up. Hers is made of a cushioned vinyl to make long days on her feet less strenuous.

(Opposite) This work space has a pincushion right at hand so Freddy always has them when she needs them. The plastic storage drawers to the right of her sewing machine also hold supplies that are often used when sewing.

stored against the wall. This will create extra space for other activities in the room when it is not being used for quilting.

The area in which you keep your sewing machine should be neat and clutter-free. Keep thread organized with a spinning thread caddy or other thread holder. A bulletin board placed on the wall can be used to hang scissors, rotary cutters, or instructions for a project that you are currently working on. Purchase a small plastic storage container or an old jewelry box with several compartments. Use the partitioned areas to store needles, thimbles, buttons, embroidery floss cards, etc.

(Opposite and this page) Small containers on top of the rolling table keep pins, scissors, and other tools in check while Freddy works.

Patterns can cause a great deal of stress in a craft area. Designate a file cabinet or several drawers to store patterns. Purchase file separators to keep various types of patterns neatly organized. If you do not particularly like filing, purchase binders with clear page protectors into which patterns can be tucked.

Keeping a small library in your quilting area can be very beneficial. Not only do books provide patterns to emulate and inspiration for creating your own original quilts, they offer a mini vacation from working. Although quilting is a very enjoyable craft, it can cause strain on your eyes, neck, or fingers due to the small tools used, as well as having to bend over often for cutting. A chair covered with pillows and one of your own quilt creations will offer you a place to sit and relax for a few moments, without ever having to leave your craft space.

(Right) This closet, tucked away in the hallway, adds even more storage. Freddy's fabric is plentiful, so she needs quite a lot of room.

(Opposite) This "library" is a nice retreat from work. There are plenty of books to inspire and a great chair in which to enjoy them.

Other Ideas

(Opposite) This sliding wall is made from a special fiber composite so that Freddy can pin fabric in various places while she is designing.

(Top left) A cork wall is great for pinning fabric samples within view. This way, you never have to sort through your stash to see what is available to you.

(Top right) Plastic bins filled with thread, sorted by color, make it quite easy to access the desired colors.

(Left) Another great way to display fabric samples is by having them stored in binders. Lining them up on a shelf makes it easy to browse colors, patterns, and textures.

141

Metric Equivalency

mm-millimeters   cm-centimeters

inches to millimeters and centimeters

inches	mm	cm	inches	cm	inches	cm
⅛	3	0.3	9	22.9	30	76.2
¼	6	0.6	10	25.4	31	78.7
½	13	1.3	12	30.5	33	83.8
⅝	16	1.6	13	33.0	34	86.4
¾	19	1.9	14	35.6	35	88.9
⅞	22	2.2	15	38.1	36	91.4
1	25	2.5	16	40.6	37	94.0
1¼	32	3.2	17	43.2	38	96.5
1½	38	3.8	18	45.7	39	99.1
1¾	44	4.4	19	48.3	40	101.6
2	51	5.1	20	50.8	41	104.1
2½	64	6.4	21	53.3	42	106.7
3	76	7.6	22	55.9	43	109.2
3½	89	8.9	23	58.4	44	111.8
4	102	10.2	24	61.0	45	114.3
4½	114	11.4	25	63.5	46	116.8
5	127	12.7	26	66.0	47	119.4
6	152	15.2	27	68.6	48	121.9
7	178	17.8	28	71.1	49	124.5
8	203	20.3	29	73.7	50	127.0

Credits

Book Editor: Ana Maria Ventura

Book Designer: Dan Emerson for Pinnacle Marketing

Production Designer: Richie Taylor

Photographers:

Ryne Hazen and Zac Williams for Chapelle, Ltd.

Steve Aja Photography (Anna Corba's studio)

Brian Oglesbee (Suze Weinberg's studio)

Mark Tanner Photography (Dee Gruenig and Linda Woodward's studios)

About the Author

Jo Packham has been one of the most notable figures in the creative industry for more than 25 years. She is the owner of the publishing company Chapelle, Ltd., a 25-year-old Utah corporation that authors, packages, and copublishes successful coffee table, instructional, and gift publications, ranging from home decoration and gardening to master woodworking and antique needlework. With over 300 titles, Chapelle is the premier publisher of arts-and-crafts books, and today, works solely for Sterling Publishing, a division of Barnes and Noble. Jo herself has authored over 20 titles, including the two best-selling publications *Decorate Rich* and *Extraordinary Touches for an Ordinary Day*.

Jo with her daughter Sara Toliver has also created a one-of-a-kind arts-and-crafts symposimun, WomenCreate. Taking place on Historic 25th Street in Ogden, Utah, WomenCreate™ includes classes and workshops showcasing the industry's top artists in over 30 different craft mediums. Taking place annually over the course of 54 days WomenCreate includes events from a Women Who Create Brunch to book signings to concerts in the park.

Jo is also the co-owner with her daughter of Ogden, Utah-based

retail stores Ruby and Begonia, The White Fig, and Olive & Dahlia, located on Historic 25th Street. Her untiring dedication brings to every endeavor a commitment of excellence and success.

Index

Air Element or Orange Personality, The 36
Anna Corba 102–109
Adventurer, The 27, 29
Armoire 100
Arrange by Category 47
Beading 110–121
Beads 112–116
Books 40
Budget Considerations 17–19
Ceiling Storage 52
Choosing Color Combinations 38
Clasps and Findings 117

Closet Organizers 94–97
Counter Space 52
Decorating Style Assessment 24–32
Drawer Space 47
Earth Element or Blue Personality, The 36
Embellishments 126–129
Fabrics 124, 132–141

Fibers 124
Fire Element or Red Personality, The 36
Floor Plan and Space Options 20–22
Foreword 5
Galichia, Gina 63
Guardian, The 27, 31
General Organizing Solutions 47–53
Genovese, Sandi 90–91
Getting Started 10–55
Gruenig, Dee 72–75
Idealist, The 27–28
Ink Pads 68
Introduction 8–9
Leader, The 27, 30
Magazines 41
Making the Most of a Small Space 120–121
Maximizing Cabinet Space 48
Moran, Freddy 14, 132–141
Organizational Maintenance 54
Paper Crafts 92–109
Papers and Cardstocks 82–85
Patterns 125–126
Personality Assessment 32–37
Plan of Action 13–16
Quilting 130–141
Recommended Spacing Allowances 22–23
Ribbon 43
Rothamel, Susan Pickering 76–79
Rubber Stamping and Stenciling 66–79
Scrapbooking 80–91
Shelves 47, 99
Stack Wisely 49
Stained Glass and Mosaics 56–65
Stamps and Stencils 68
Storage Boxes 87, 98–101
Storage Problems and Solutions 39–42
Tips for Healthier Crafting 55
Tools and Supplies 119, 126
Wall Storage 50
Water Element or White Personality, The 37
Weinberg, Suze 70–71
Wire 117–118
Woodward, Linda 64–65
Work Surface 100
Yarn Crafts and Needlework 122–129